# Jack Johnson

## SLEEP THROUGH THE STATIC

This book is printed on recycled paper. The CD *Sleep Through the Static* was recorded 100% on solar energy.

This book was approved by Jack Johnson

Photography by Thomas Campbell

Piano/vocal arrangements by John Nicholas

**Cherry Lane Music Company**
Director of Publications/Project Editor: Mark Phillips
Manager of Publications: Gabrielle Fastman

ISBN: 978-1-60378-055-1

*Visit our website at www.cherrylane.com*

## A LETTER FROM JACK:

*To whom it may concern:*

*My friends and I have just finished recording a new album called* Sleep Through the Static. *At this point in my life I weigh about 190 pounds and my ear hairs are getting longer. I also have a couple of kids. My wife popped them out, but I helped. Some of the songs on this album are about making babies. Some of the songs are about raising them. Some of the songs are about the world that these children will grow up in—a world of war and love, and hate, and time and space. Some of the songs are about saying goodbye to people I love and will miss.*

*We recorded the songs onto analog tape machines powered by the sun in Hawaii and Los Angeles. One day, JP Plunier walked into the studio and told us, "It has been four to six feet and glassy for long enough," and so we gave him a variety of wind and rain as well as sun and so on. And Robert Carranza helped to put it all in the right places.*

*After inviting Zach Gill to join Adam Topol, Merlo Podlewski, and me on our last world tour, we decided to make him an official member of our gang. So our gang now has a piano player, which probably makes us much less intimidating, but Merlo, our bass player, is six-foot-three, so we are still confident.*

*All of these songs have been on my mind for a while and it is nice to share them. I am continually grateful to my wife, who is typing this letter as I dictate it to her.*

*I hope you enjoy this song book.*

*Mahalo for listening,*

*Jack Johnson*

# CONTENTS

# All at Once

Words and Music by
Jack Johnson

you and the feel - ing lost and found _ you a - gain, _ a feel - ing that we have no con - trol. _

A - round the sun _ some say it's gon - na be _ the new hell. _

Some say it's still too ear - ly to tell. _ Some say it real - ly ain't _ no myth at all. _

We keep ask - ing our - selves, _ are _ we real - ly _

strong e - nough? ___ There's so man - y things ___ that ___ we got ___

___ too proud ___ of, _____ too proud of, ___

___ too proud of. ___ I want to take ___

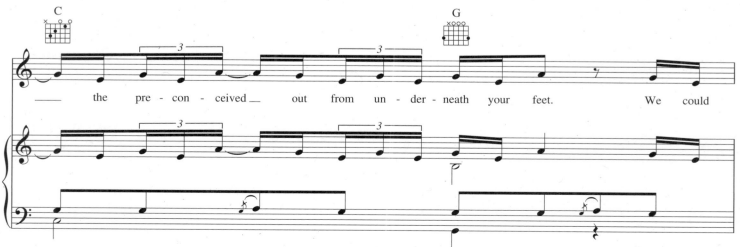

___ the pre - con - ceived ___ out from un - der - neath your feet. We could

6

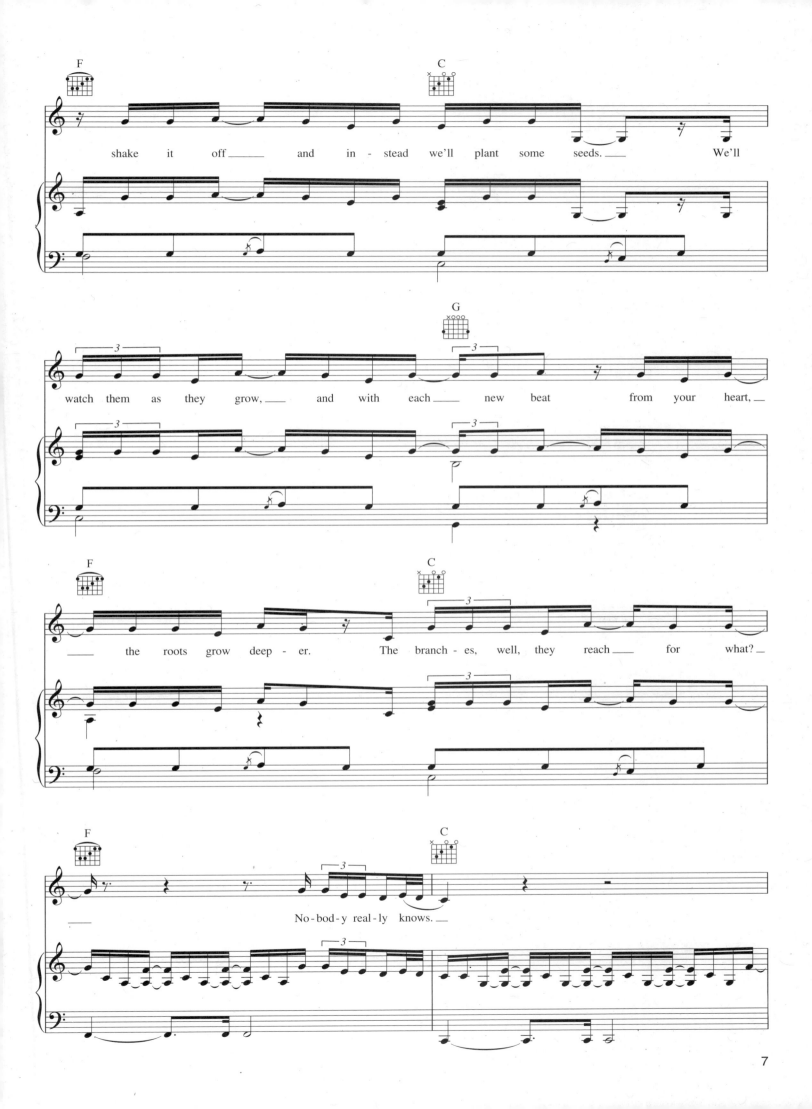

But un-der-neath it all ____ there's this heart ____ all a-lone. ____

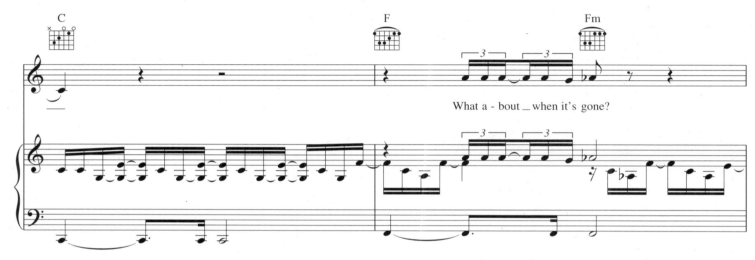

What a-bout __ when it's gone?

It real-ly won't be so long. ____ Some-times it

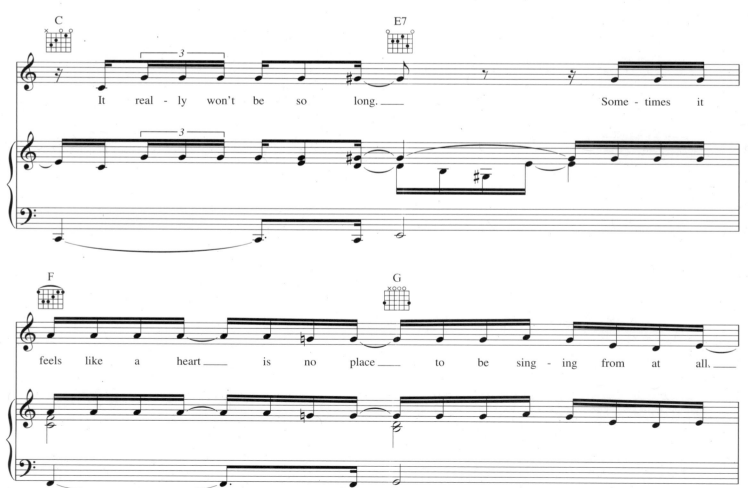

feels like a heart ____ is no place ____ to be sing-ing from at all. ____

wait-ing on the wind, ___ don't for-get to breathe, ___ 'cause as the

dark - ness gets deep - er, we're sink - ing, so we reach ___ for love. ___

___ At least some-thing we can hold. ___

But I'll reach ___ to you ___ from where time ___ just can't

# Sleep Through the Static

Words and Music by
Jack Johnson

yond where we should have gone. _____ Stuck _

_____ be - tween chan - nels, my thoughts _ all _____ quit. I thought a -

bout them too much, _____ al - lowed them to touch. The feel - ings that rained _

_____ down on the plains _ all dried and cracked wait - ing _____ for things that nev - er came. _ Shock an

God _____ wears _____ cam-ou-flage, _____ cries at night and drives a Dodge. _____

Pick up the beat and stop hog-ging the feast. That's no way to treat an en-e-my. _____ We'll, might-y,

might-y ap-pe-tite, we just eat 'em up and keep on driv-ing.

Free-dom can be freez-ing; take a pic-ture from the pret-ty side.

yond    where    we    should    have    gone, _____         be - yond    where    we    should    have

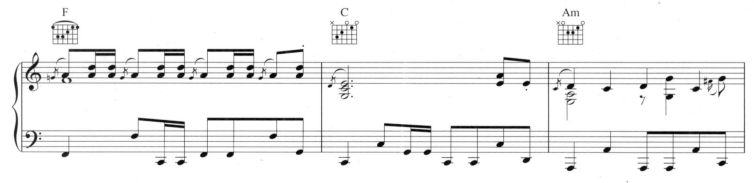

gone. _____

# Hope

Words and Music by
Jack Johnson and Zach Rogue

do. Do you think that you're not a - lone? \_\_ You real - ly think that you're im -

mune to... It's gon - na get the best of you. \_\_ It's gon - na lift you up then

let you down. \_\_ Mm, mm, mm. _____ It will de -

feat you then teach you to get back up af - ter it

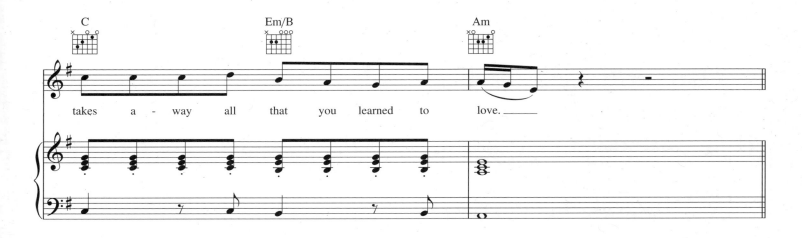

takes a-way all that you learned to love. _____

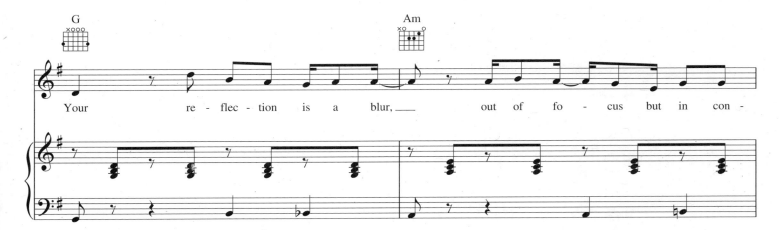

Your re-flec-tion is a blur, ___ out of fo-cus but in con-

fu-sion, the frames the sun did burn ___ at the end of a roll of de-

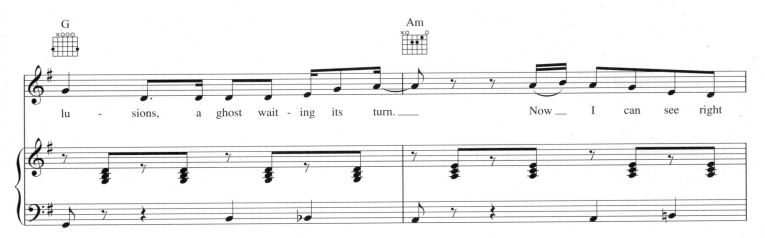

lu-sions, a ghost wait-ing its turn. ___ Now ___ I can see right

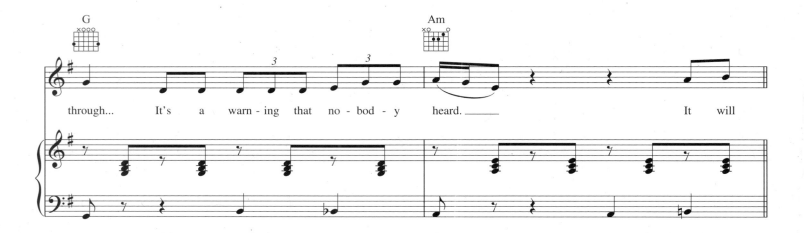

through... It's a warn-ing that no-bod-y heard. \_\_\_\_\_ It will

teach you to love what you're a-fraid of af-ter it
takes a-way all that you've learned to love, it will de-

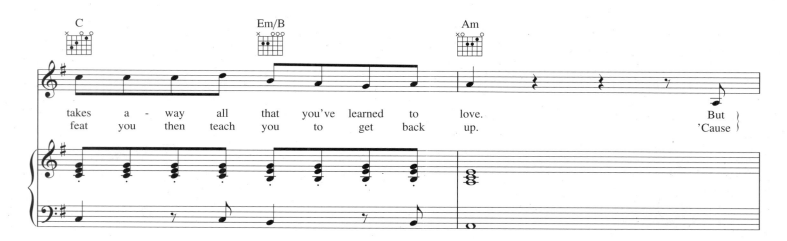

takes a-way all that you've learned to love. But
feat you then teach you to get back up. 'Cause

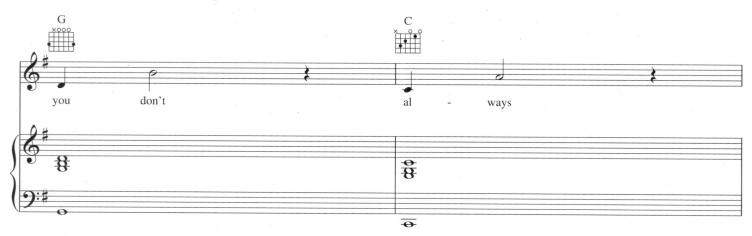

you don't al - ways

You bet-ter hope you're not a - lone.___ You bet-ter be hop-ing you're not so...

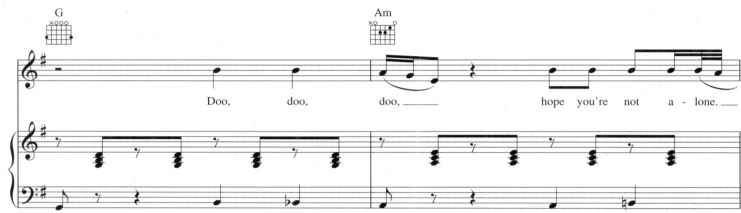

Doo, doo, doo,_____ hope you're not a - lone.___

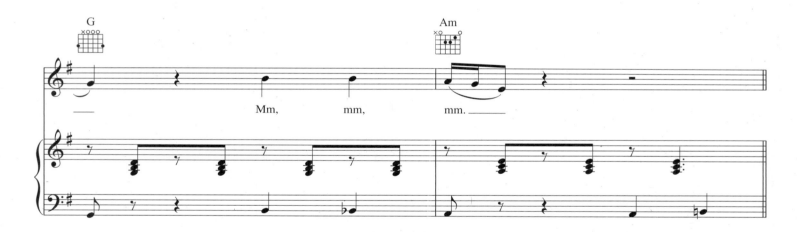

Mm, mm, mm._____

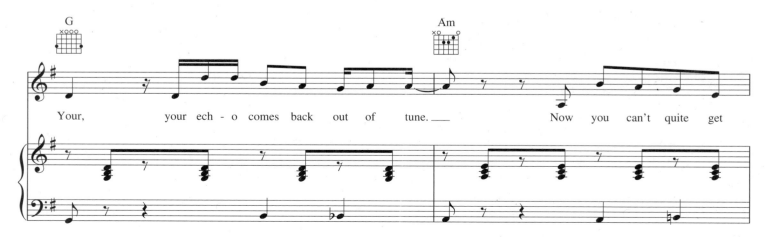

Your, your ech - o comes back out of tune.___ Now you can't quite get

# Angel

Words and Music by
Jack Johnson

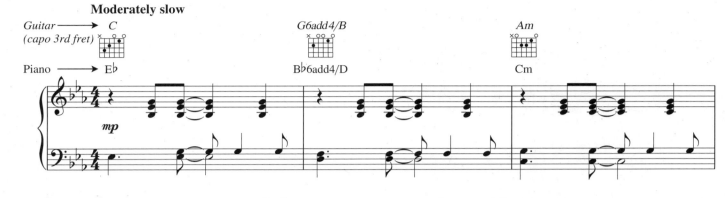

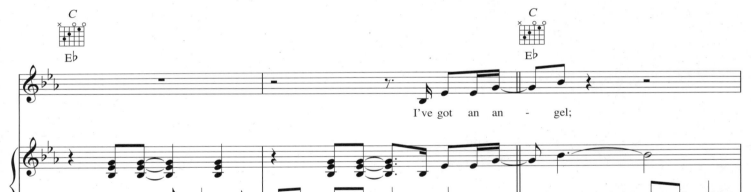

I've got an an - gel;

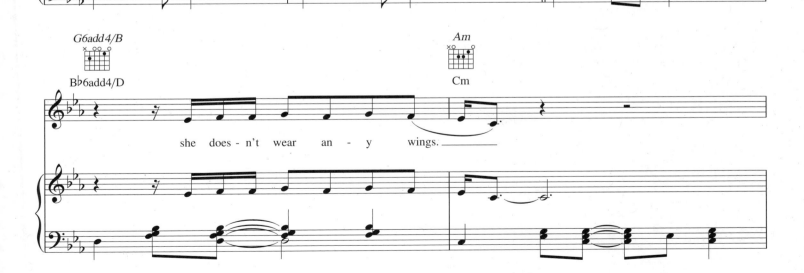

she does-n't wear an-y wings. _____

She gives me ev - 'ry-thing I could wish _ for; she gives me kiss-

es on the lips just for com - ing _____ home.

She can make an - gels;

seen it with my _____ own _____ eyes. _____

You've got to be care - ful when you've got good love, 'cause them an -

gels will __ just keep __ on mul - ti - ply - ing.

But you're so bus - y chang - ing the world. __

Just one smile __ and you could change all of mine. __

# Enemy

Words and Music by
Jack Johnson

they were mine ___ all a - long. ___
don't ___ want ___ to ___ see. ___
I ___ can't ___ ex - plain. ___

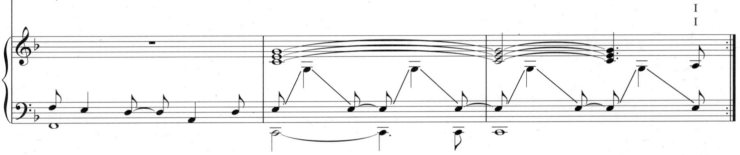

So I took it a - part, ___ built a bil - lion box - es;

there was on - ly one key. ___

You might think___ I'm your___ en - e - my, but that don't make___ you___ mine.___

___ And all I have___ now is___ em - pa - thy. I

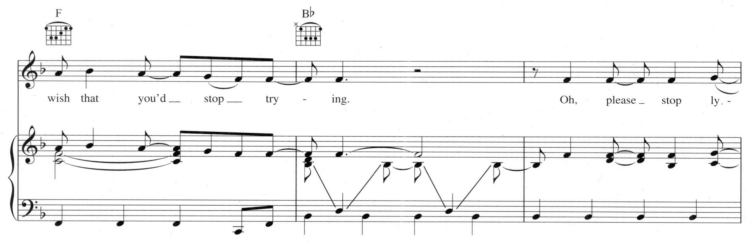

wish that you'd___ stop___ try - ing.   Oh, please___ stop ly - 

*To Coda*

ing.___   Stop.   La la la___ la la___

la la. La la la la.

Put

ha - tred in a box, then I locked it; strong - est one I made.
bur - ied all, grew a tree with - out thorns, sat be - neath its shade.

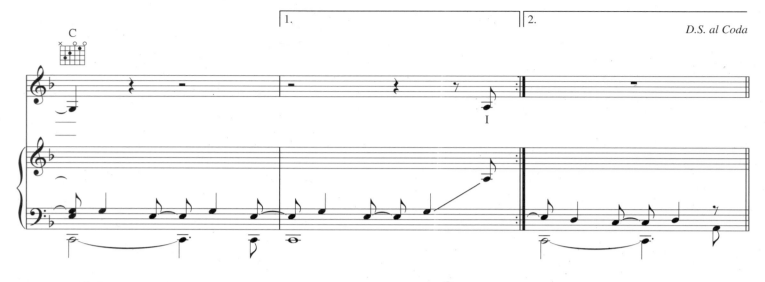

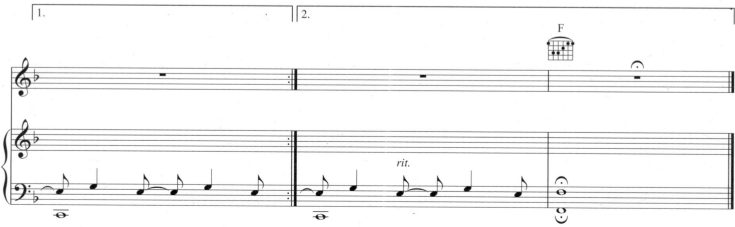

# If I Had Eyes

Words and Music by
Jack Johnson

**Moderately**

If I had eyes _____ in the back of my head, I would have

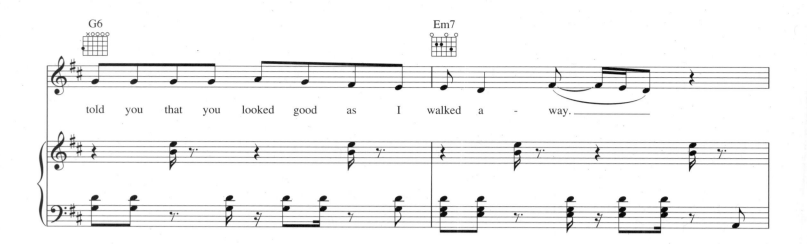

told you that you looked good as I walked a - way. _____

And if you could have tried to trust the

hand that fed, you would have nev - er been hun - gry but you'd

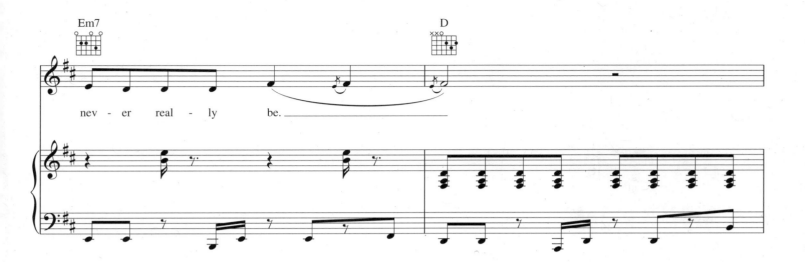

never - er real - ly be. _____

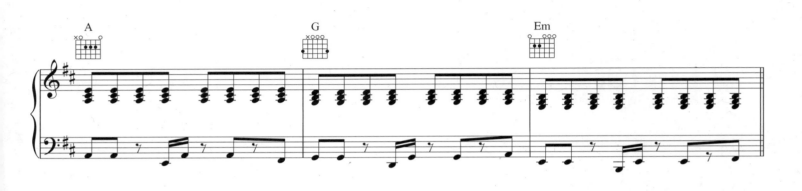

More of this or less of this or is there an - y dif - f'rence? Or

are we just hold - ing on to things that we don't have an - y -

more? _____ Some - times

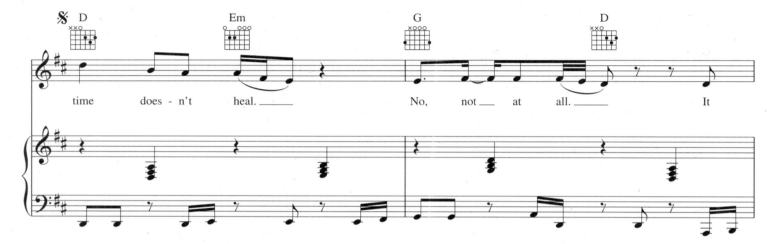

time does-n't heal. _____ No, not ___ at all. _____ It

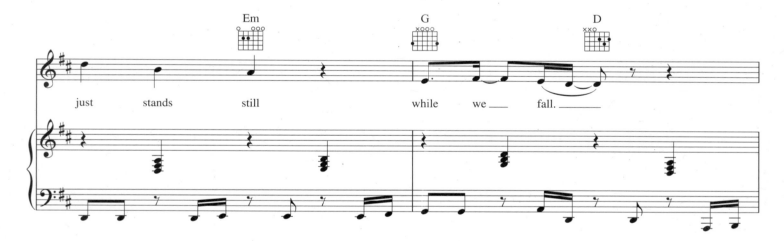

just stands still while we ___ fall. _____

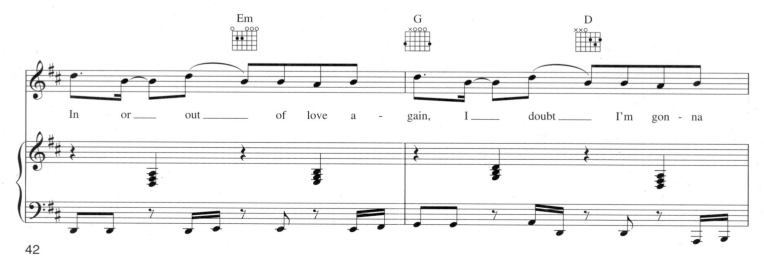

In or ___ out _____ of love a - gain, I ___ doubt ____ I'm gon - na

42

oo, _____ oo.) _____

lot of ___ peo - ple spend their time just ___ float - ing.

We were ___ vic - tims, _____ to - geth - er ___ but lone - ly. ___

You've got ___ hun - gry eyes that just can't ___ look for - ward. Can't

44

give them __ e - nough, but __ we just can't __ start o - ver.

Build - ing __ with bent nails, __ we're fall - ing __ but hold - ing. __

I don't __ want __ to take up an - y __ more __ of __ your

*D.S. al Coda*

time.         Time, __ time, time. __ Some - times

# Same Girl

Words and Music by
Jack Johnson

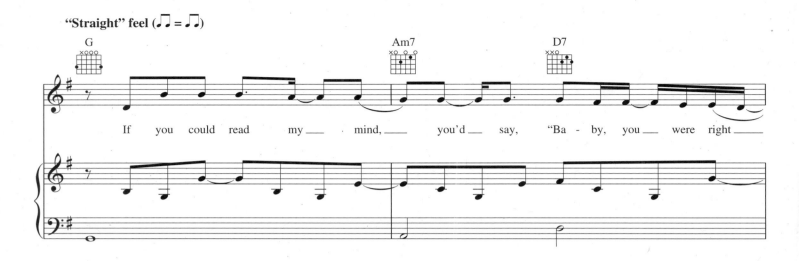

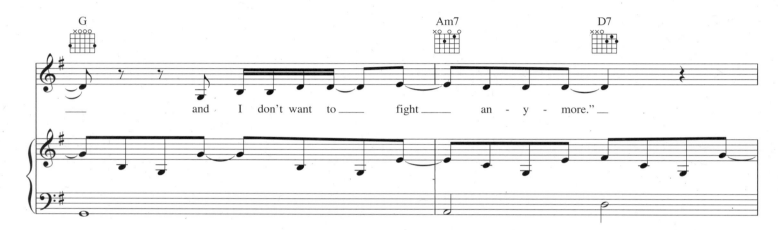

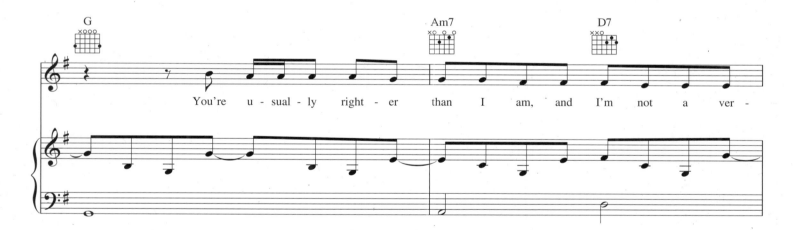

48

you.　So let's be through ＿

＿ with this ＿ one, ＿　'cause some things nev - er

change.　I know you're still my

same　girl ＿＿＿　who builds her own frames ＿

for the pic - tures that she paints; __ the lights in Mon - te - rey __

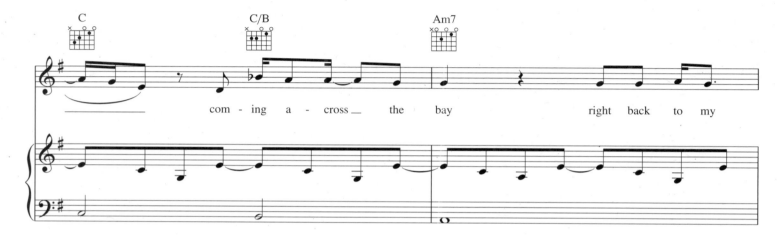

__ com - ing a - cross __ the bay right back to my

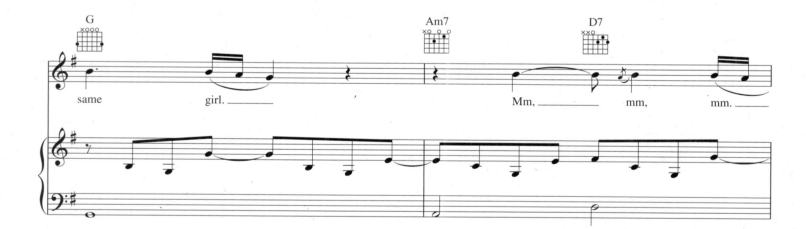

same girl. _____ Mm, _____ mm, mm. _____

__ Mm, _____ mm, mm,

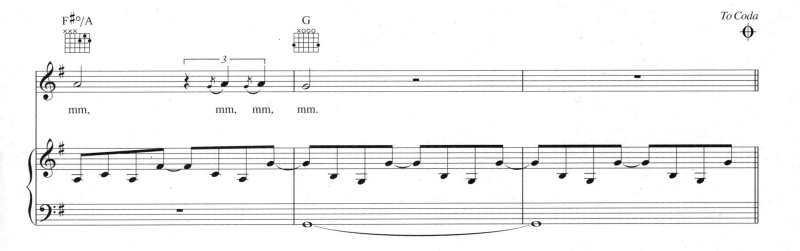

mm,                    mm,    mm,    mm.

How can you be so ___ calm ___ when the truth ___ is that some -

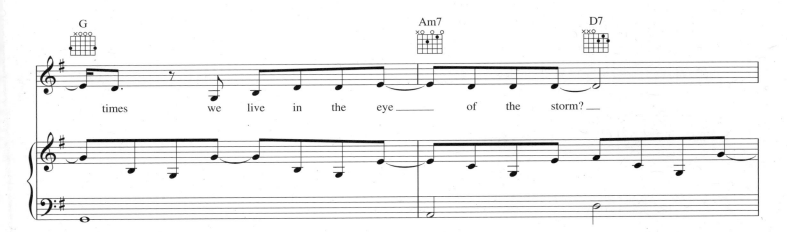

times    we  live  in  the  eye ___ of  the  storm? ___

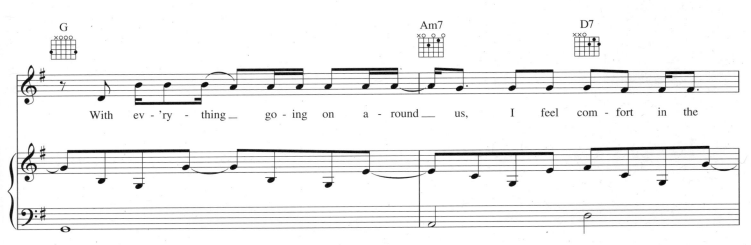

With ev - 'ry - thing ___ go - ing  on  a - round ___ us,  I  feel  com - fort  in  the

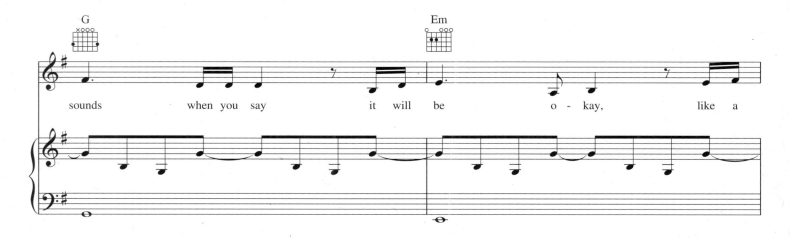

sounds when you say it will be o - kay, like a

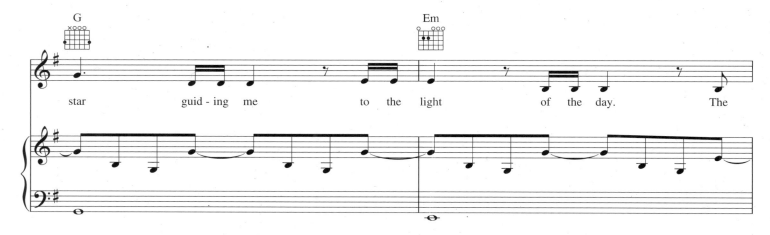

star guid - ing me to the light of the day. The

*D.S. al Coda*

dol - drums could fol - low me, _____ but not with my

Mm, _____ mm, mm, mm, _____ mm, mm, mm.

# What You Thought You Need

Words and Music by
Jack Johnson

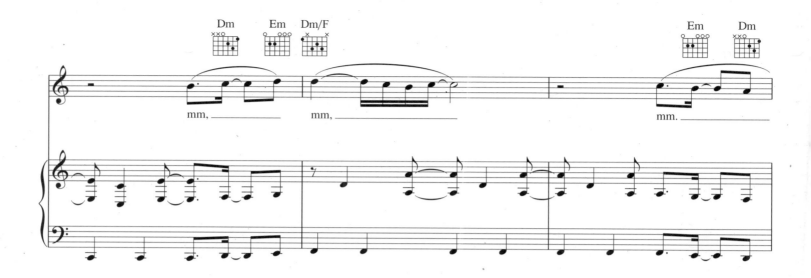

mm, _____ mm, _____ mm. _____

Well,

54

I can't give you ev - 'ry - thing _ you want, _____ but
We can park the van and walk _ to town, _____ find the
I will make the ta - ble in - to a bed. _____ The

I could give _ you what _ you thought _ you need. _____ A
cheap-est bot - tle of wine _ that we ____ could find ____ and
can - dle is burn-ing down; _ it's time ____ to rest. _____ I can't

map to keep _ be - neath your seat _ you'll read ____ to me; _ in time _ I'll get _ you there. _
talk a - bout ____ the road _ be - hind, how get - ting lost _ is not _ a waste _ of time. _
take back things _ al - read - y gone, _ but I could give _ you prom - is - es ____ for keeps. _

But
*Le*
And I would

fold it up __ so we __ don't find __ our way __ back soon; __ no - bod - y knows __ we're here. __
*bois d'a - mour* __ will take __ us home; __ in the mo - ment we __ will sing __ as the for - est sleeps. __
on - ly take __ them back __ if they __ be - come __ your own __ and you __ give them __ to me. __

1.

It's all _____ for the sake ___
And it's all _____

_____ of ar - riv - ing ___ with _____ you.

Well, it's all _____ for the sake ___

make us in - to an - y-thing; it could make us grow __ and be - come what __ we'll be. __

Mm. __

How {will}{can} we real - ly know? __ It's just like __ it

# Adrift

Words and Music by
Jack Johnson

Lyrics:

Your voice is a-drift; I _____ can't ex-pect it to sing to
This was a scene worth _____ wak-ing up for. When I
Your voice is your own; I _____ can't pro-tect it. You'll have to

me _____ as if I _____ was the on-ly one. _____
woke up you plant-ed _____ me in my own pot. _____
sing _____ a verse no _____ one has ev-er known. _

I'll fol - low ___ you, ___ a  
Don't know ___ why, ___ but  
Don't be a - fraid ___ 'cause

leaf that's fol - low - ing the sun. ___  
some - how it just feels so wrong. ___  
no one ev - er sings a - lone. ___

When will my weight ___ be too much for you?  
When you set, ___ I will be lone - ly.  
Your weight will nev - er be too much for me.

When will these i - deas _____ real - ly be my own? _____
But when you rise _____ a - gain, I'll have be - come the
Your i - deas _____ have _____ al - ways been your own. _____

_____ sun.
_____ 'Cause this mo - ment keeps on mov - ing;
_____ I will shine down up - on you
And this mo - ment keeps on mov - ing;

*Play 3 times*

we were nev - er meant ___ to hold on. _____
as if you were ___ the on - ly one.
we were nev - er meant ___ to hold on. _____

*Begin fade*

*Fade out*

*p*

64

# Go On

Words and Music by
Jack Johnson

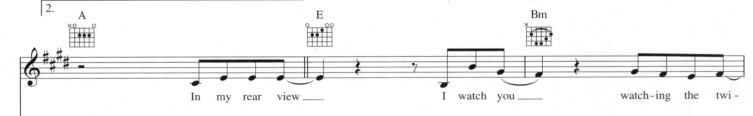

In my rear view ____ I watch you ____ watch-ing the twi-

light be - hind the tel - e - phone ____ lines ____ with noth - ing to prove ____

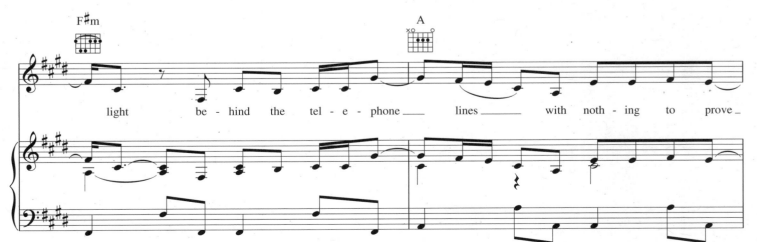

place that I ___ can't be, ___ but there's no a-pol-o-gies. ___ Just go on, ___

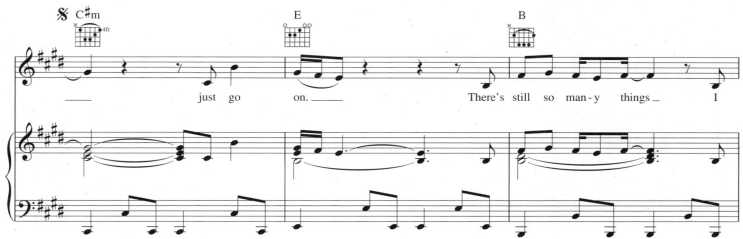

___ just go on. ___ There's still so man-y things ___ I

wan-na say to you, ___ but go on, ___ just go on. ___ We're bound ___

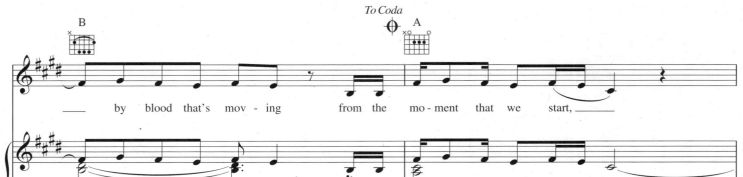

___ by blood that's mov-ing from the mo-ment that we start, ___

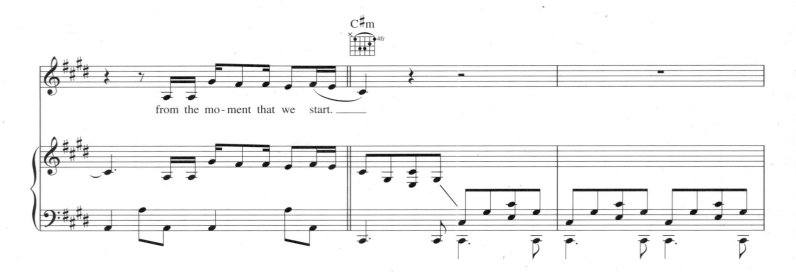

from the mo - ment that we start. _____

I see your per -

fect lit - tle eyes       watch the shad - ows of ___ the clouds ___ on the

F#m ... to let it ___ go? ___ Live vi - car - i - ous - ly through

A

E you could do the same; ___ it's the least you could do. ___ 'Cause it's a ___ lone -

Bm

F#m ly lit - tle chain if you don't add to it. So go on, ___

A

D.S. al Coda

Coda A mo - ment that ___ we start. Just go on, ___ just go

C#m

70

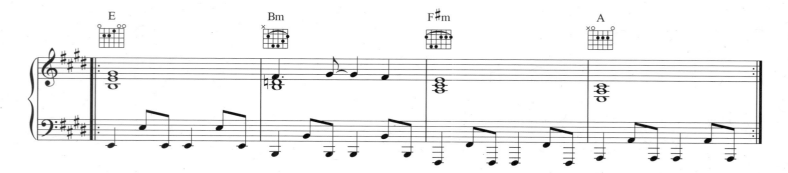

# They Do, They Don't

Words and Music by
Jack Johnson

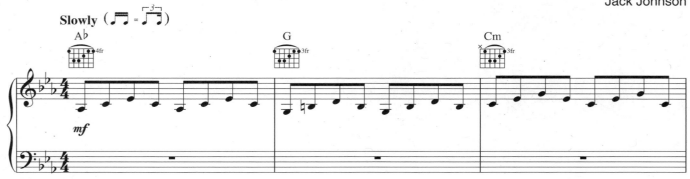

73

Tied down a-gainst __ the tracks, __ scream-ing in si - lent black __ __ and...Why'd __ you trust __ us? We are such vil - lains. We would tell our - selves __ __ an - y - thing __ we want to hear if we are will - ing. To lis - ten is __ to learn, __

__ then too much is what we de - serve. __ And how come when we say that we do, __

we don't? Pray to an-y-bod-y you want; \_\_ we won't. Oh, oh, oh, oh, oh, oh,

oh. But if we're the ones to blame, then the fruit \_\_ should-n't taste so good. We were u-

u-used to think-ing we got noth-ing to lose. \_\_ We're los-ing ev-'ry-thing but the tru-

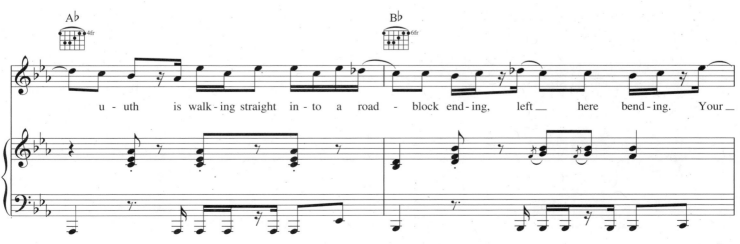

u-uth is walk-ing straight in-to a road-block end-ing, left \_\_ here bend-ing. Your \_\_

point of view was cho - sen by the ser-pent's ruse.

With all __ its dos __ and don'ts, __ the fu - ture's an emp - ty prom -

ise, un - con - cerned __ and so ti - red of wait - ing. We could sell it wood - en

hors - es full __ of night - mares. And when __ they o - pen, __ this all __ might re - com - pose. __

u - uth is walk-ing straight in-to a road - block end-ing, left ___ here bend-ing. Your ___

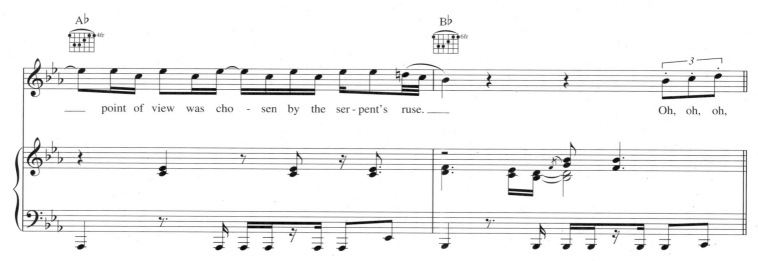

___ point of view was cho - sen by the ser-pent's ruse. ___ Oh, oh, oh,

oh.
*(Sing 1st time only)*

# While We Wait

Words and Music by
Jack Johnson

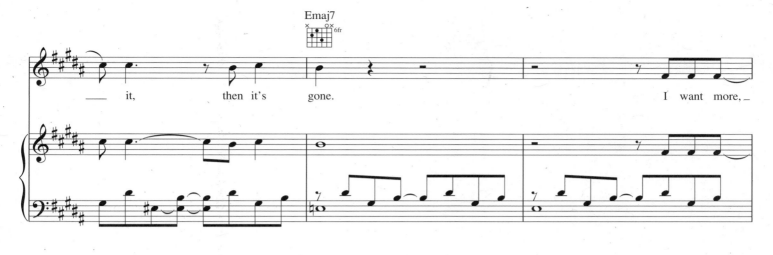

it,     then it's    gone.                            I want more, ___

___                                 more     and     more.

And   if   you _____ steal the fire, ___              give me

some.                                   'Cause the sun ___

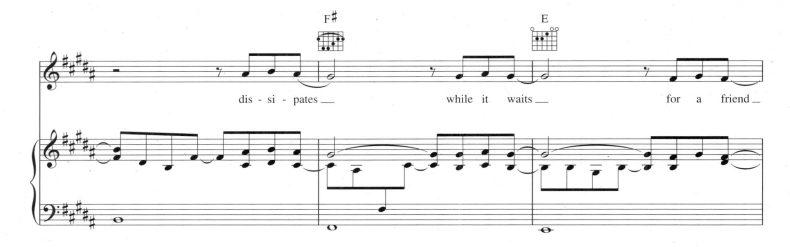

dis - si - pates ___ while it waits ___ for a friend ___

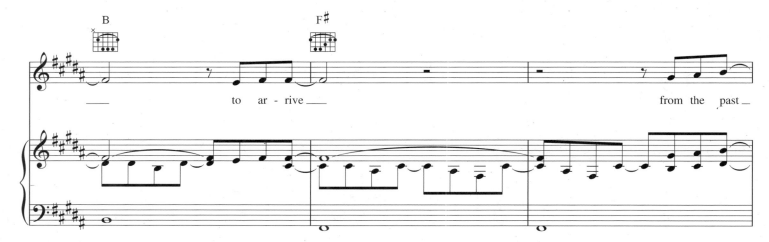

to ar - rive ___ from the past ___

while it pulls ___ us a - round ___

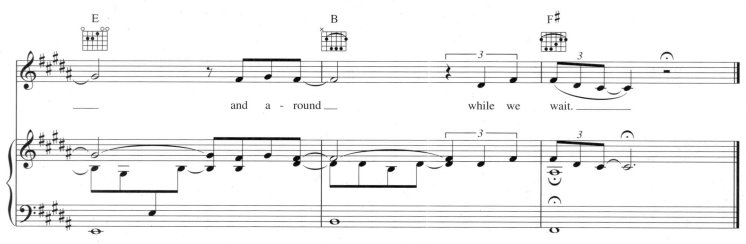

and a - round ___ while we wait. ___

# Monsoon

Words and Music by
Jack Johnson and Merlo Podlewski

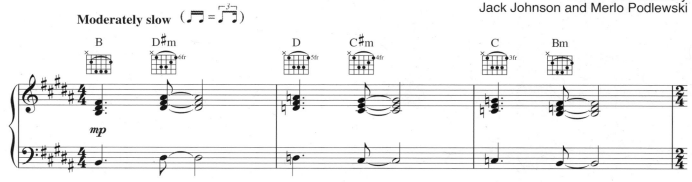

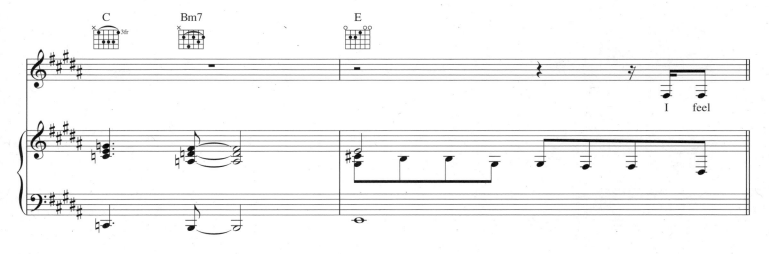

I feel

sor - row for ___ the fear ___ and ev - 'ry - thing ___ it brings; ___

won - der if it will ev - er sleep.   I

know you un - der - stand___ 'cause you brief - ly look___ a - way,___

fo - cus - ing on noth - ing, so now ev - 'ry - thing is___

clear.
plain?

'Cause there's no one to blame.___   You've got no place to hide;___
'Cause it's on - ly the pain___   com - ing straight through,___

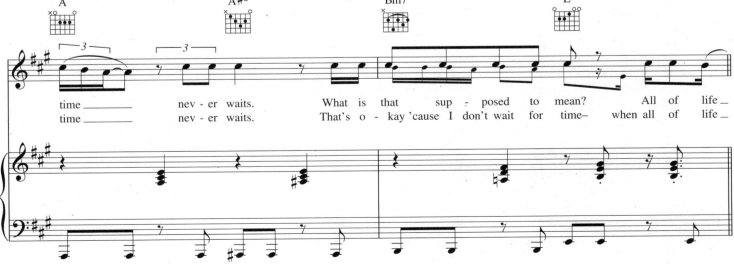

soon - er or lat - er they'll weep their way back to the sea. Gon - na fi - n'lly be

free; you're free for a while, un - til they

break, like waves of sor - row al - ways do. All in due

time, 'cause time nev - er waits.

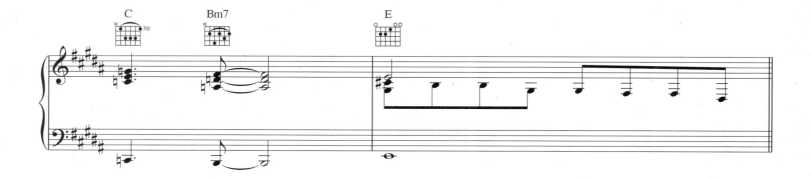

Dad - dy, don't __ day - dream a - gain; __ just help me to be - lieve __ and then __

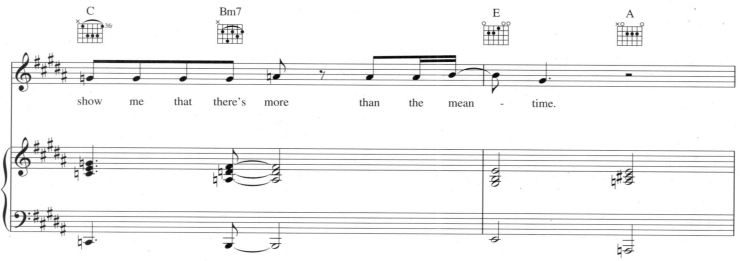

show me that there's more than the mean - time.

Son - ny, do you hear the sound? __ You will feel it when __ it breaks. __ You will

D.S. al Coda

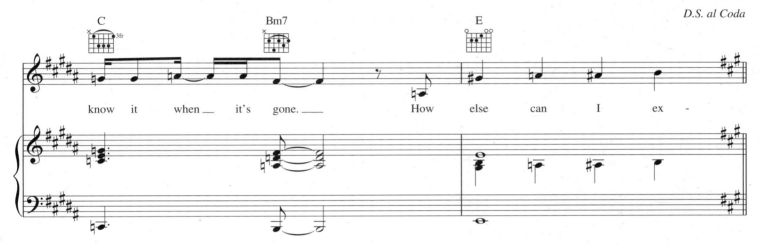

know it when __ it's gone. __ How else can I ex -

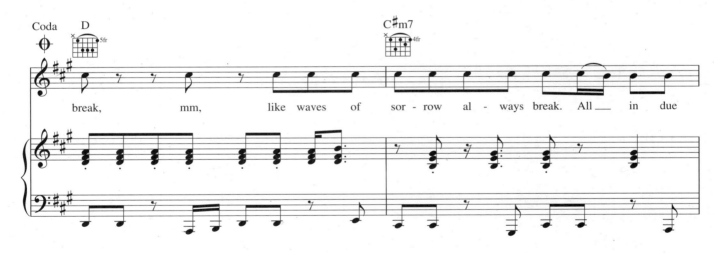

break, mm, like waves of sor - row al - ways break. All __ in due

time, __ 'cause time __ nev - er waits. __

89

# Losing Keys

Words and Music by
Jack Johnson

So come and tell me some-thing __ that you've al-read-y told __

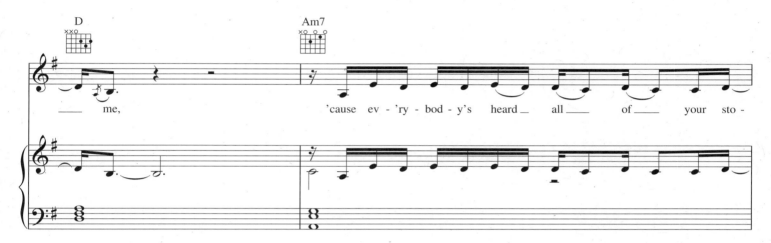

__ me, 'cause ev-'ry-bod-y's heard __ all __ of __ your sto-

ries. I hope that some of them are true. __

I've been

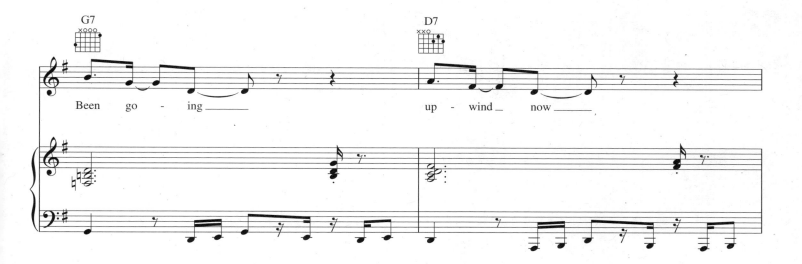

Been go - ing _____ up - wind _ now _____

for too _ long; _____ for - get _ how _____ to let _ go. _____

*D.S. al Coda*

Seems too _ hard, _____ too late _ now _____ to turn a - round. _

*D.S.S. and fade*

Coda  G

# More Great Piano/Vocal Books

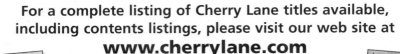

## FROM CHERRY LANE

For a complete listing of Cherry Lane titles available,
including contents listings, please visit our web site at

**www.cherrylane.com**

02500343 Almost Famous . . . . . . . . . . . . . $14.95
02502171 The Best of Boston . . . . . . . . . . $17.95
02500672 Black Eyed Peas – Elephunk . . . $17.95
02500665 Sammy Cahn Songbook . . . . . . . $24.95
02500144 Mary Chapin Carpenter –
        Party Doll & Other Favorites . . $16.95
02502163 Mary Chapin Carpenter –
        Stones in the Road . . . . . . . . . . $17.95
02502165 John Denver Anthology –
        Revised . . . . . . . . . . . . . . . . $22.95
02502227 John Denver –
        A Celebration of Life. . . . . . $14.95
02500002 John Denver Christmas . . . . . . . $14.95
02502166 John Denver's Greatest Hits . . . . $17.95
02502151 John Denver – A Legacy
        in Song (Softcover) . . . . . . . . $24.95
02502152 John Denver – A Legacy
        in Song (Hardcover) . . . . . . . . $34.95
02500566 Poems, Prayers and Promises: The Art
        and Soul of John Denver . . . . . $19.95
02500326 John Denver –
        The Wildlife Concert . . . . . . . $17.95
02500501 John Denver and the Muppets:
        A Christmas Together . . . . . . . . $9.95
02509922 The Songs of Bob Dylan . . . . . . $29.95
02500586 Linda Eder – Broadway My Way $14.95
02500497 Linda Eder – Gold. . . . . . . . . . . $14.95
02500396 Linda Eder –
        Christmas Stays the Same . . . . $17.95
02500175 Linda Eder –
        It's No Secret Anymore. . . . . . $14.95
02502209 Linda Eder – It's Time. . . . . . . . $17.95
02500630 Donald Fagen – 5 of the Best . . . $7.95
02500535 Erroll Garner Anthology . . . . . . $19.95
02500270 Gilbert & Sullivan for Easy Piano $12.95
02500318 Gladiator. . . . . . . . . . . . . . . . . . $12.95
02500273 Gold & Glory:
        The Road to El Dorado . . . . . . $16.95
02502126 Best of Guns N' Roses . . . . . . . . $17.95
02502072 Guns N' Roses – Selections from
        Use Your Illusion I and II . . . . $17.95
02500014 Sir Roland Hanna Collection . . . $19.95
02500352 Hanson – This Time Around . . . $16.95
02502134 Best of Lenny Kravitz . . . . . . . . $12.95
02500012 Lenny Kravitz – 5. . . . . . . . . . . $16.95
02500381 Lenny Kravitz – Greatest Hits . . . $14.95
02503701 Man of La Mancha. . . . . . . . . . . $10.95

02500693 Dave Matthews – Some Devil. . . $16.95
02500555 Dave Matthews Band –
        Busted Stuff . . . . . . . . . . . . . . $16.95
02500003 Dave Matthews Band – Before
        These Crowded Streets . . . . . $17.95
02502199 Dave Matthews Band – Crash . . $17.95
02500390 Dave Matthews Band –
        Everyday . . . . . . . . . . . . . . . . $14.95
02500493 Dave Matthews Band – Live in Chicago
        12/19/98 at the United Center . $14.95
02502192 Dave Matthews Band – Under
        the Table and Dreaming. . . . . . $17.95
02500681 John Mayer – Heavier Things . . $16.95
02500563 John Mayer – Room for Squares $16.95
02500081 Natalie Merchant – Ophelia. . . . $14.95
02500423 Natalie Merchant – Tigerlily . . . $14.95
02502895 Nine. . . . . . . . . . . . . . . . . . . . . $17.95
02500425 Time and Love: The Art and
        Soul of Laura Nyro. . . . . . . . . $19.95
02502204 The Best of Metallica. . . . . . . . . $17.95
02500407 O-Town . . . . . . . . . . . . . . . . . . $14.95
02500010 Tom Paxton – The Honor
        of Your Company. . . . . . . . . . $17.95
02507962 Peter, Paul & Mary –
        Holiday Concert . . . . . . . . . . . $17.95
02500145 Pokemon 2.B.A. Master. . . . . . . $12.95
02500026 The Prince of Egypt . . . . . . . . . $16.95
02500660 Best of Bonnie Raitt. . . . . . . . . . $17.95
02502189 The Bonnie Raitt Collection . . . $22.95
02502230 Bonnie Raitt – Fundamental . . . $17.95
02502139 Bonnie Raitt –
        Longing in Their Hearts . . . . . . $16.95
02502088 Bonnie Raitt – Luck of the Draw $14.95
02507958 Bonnie Raitt – Nick of Time . . . $14.95
02502190 Bonnie Raitt – Road Tested. . . . $24.95
02502218 Kenny Rogers – The Gift . . . . . . $16.95
02500072 Saving Private Ryan . . . . . . . . . . $14.95
02500197 SHeDAISY –
        The Whole SHeBANG . . . . . . . $14.95
02500414 Shrek. . . . . . . . . . . . . . . . . . . . . $14.95
02500536 Spirit – Stallion of the Cimarron $16.95
02500166 Steely Dan – Anthology . . . . . . $17.95
02500622 Steely Dan –
        Everything Must Go . . . . . . . . $14.95
02500284 Steely Dan –
        Two Against Nature . . . . . . . . $14.95
02500165 Best of Steely Dan . . . . . . . . . . $14.95

02500344 Billy Strayhorn:
        An American Master. . . . . . . . $17.95
02502132 Barbra Streisand –
        Back to Broadway . . . . . . . . . $19.95
02500515 Barbra Streisand –
        Christmas Memories . . . . . . . . $16.95
02507969 Barbra Streisand – A Collection:
        Greatest Hits and More . . . . . $17.95
02502164 Barbra Streisand – The Concert $22.95
02500550 Essential Barbra Streisand. . . . . $24.95
02502228 Barbra Streisand –
        Higher Ground. . . . . . . . . . . . $16.95
02500196 Barbra Streisand –
        A Love Like Ours . . . . . . . . . . $16.95
02500280 Barbra Streisand – Timeless . . . $19.95
02503617 John Tesh – Avalon . . . . . . . . . $15.95
02502178 The John Tesh Collection. . . . . . $17.95
02503623 John Tesh – A Family Christmas $15.95
02505511 John Tesh –
        Favorites for Easy Piano. . . . . . $12.95
02503630 John Tesh – Grand Passion . . . . $16.95
02500124 John Tesh – One World. . . . . . . $14.95
02500307 John Tesh – Pure Movies 2 . . . . $16.95
02500565 Thoroughly Modern Millie. . . . . $17.95
02500576 Toto – 5 of the Best. . . . . . . . . . $7.95
02502175 Tower of Power –
        Silver Anniversary . . . . . . . . . $17.95
02502198 The "Weird Al" Yankovic
        Anthology. . . . . . . . . . . . . . . $17.95
02502217 Trisha Yearwood –
        A Collection of Hits . . . . . . . . $16.95
02500334 Maury Yeston – December Songs $17.95
02502225 The Maury Yeston Songbook. . . $19.95

**See your local music dealer or contact:**

**CHERRY LANE**
**MUSIC COMPANY**
6 East 32nd Street, New York, NY 10016
*Quality in Printed Music*

EXCLUSIVELY DISTRIBUTED BY

**HAL•LEONARD®**
**CORPORATION**
7777 W. BLUEMOUND RD. P.O. BOX 13819 MILWAUKEE, WI 53213

Prices, contents and availability subject to change without notice.
0404